STUDY GUIDE

THAT DOESN'T JUST HAPPEN

HOW
EXCELLENCE
ACCELERATES
EVERYTHING

Copyright © 2021 by Mike Kai

Published by Inspire

All rights reserved. No portion of this book may be reproduced, stored in a retrieval system, or transmitted in any form or by any means—electronic, mechanical, photocopy, recording, scanning, or other—except for brief quotations in critical reviews or articles, without prior written permission of the author.

All scripture quotations have been taken from the Holy Bible, New International Version®, NIV®. Copyright © 1973, 1978, 1984, 2011 by Biblica, Inc.™ Used by permission of Zondervan. All rights reserved worldwide. www.zondervan.com. The "NIV" and "New International Version" are trademarks registered in the United States Patent and Trademark Office by Biblica, Inc.™
For foreign and subsidiary rights, contact the author.

Cover design by: Leanne Thomas
Photos by: Brenner Quijano

ISBN: 978-1-954089-22-8   1 2 3 4 5 6 7 8 9 10

Printed in the United States of America

STUDY GUIDE

THAT DOESN'T JUST HAPPEN

HOW EXCELLENCE ACCELERATES EVERYTHING

MIKE KAI

INSPIRE

CONTENTS

**PART 1 BUILD LIKE KING SOLOMON:
          CREATING A CULTURE OF EXCELLENCE** 7

Chapter 1. Excellence in the Process 8

Chapter 2. Excellence in the Details 14

Chapter 3. Excellence in the Curation 20

Chapter 4. Excellence in the Culture 26

**PART 2 SEE LIKE THE QUEEN OF SHEBA:
          CREATIVE ADAPTATION & CULTURAL** 33

Chapter 5. See the Hard Truths 34

Chapter 6. See the Potential 40

PART 3 FINISH BETTER: CULTIVATING LEGACY 47

Chapter 7. Build to Change 48

Chapter 8. Build to Last 54

Chapter 9. Build to Leave a Legacy 62

Chapter 10. Keep Enterprising If You Want To Keep
            Rising 68

PART 1

BUILD LIKE KING SOLOMON: CREATING A CULTURE OF EXCELLENCE

chapter 1

EXCELLENCE IN THE PROCESS

*A culture of excellence doesn't just happen.
It's intentional, and it starts with leadership.*

Reading Time

As you read Chapter 1: "Excellence in the Process" in *That Doesn't Just Happen*, review, reflect, and respond to the text by answering the following questions.

Review, Reflect, and Respond

How do you define "the process?" How would you rate your current processes?

_____
_____
_____
_____
_____
_____
_____
_____
_____
_____

What's one area your organization could improve on concerning its processes?

_____
_____
_____
_____
_____
_____
_____
_____
_____
_____

How do intentionality and processes go hand in hand?

_____
_____
_____
_____

Do you think it's important to recognize that the Queen of Sheba went out of her way to meet King Solomon? Why or why not?

_____
_____
_____
_____

Why did the Queen of Sheba spend so much time planning and preparing for the trip to meet King Solomon?

_____
_____
_____
_____

How can deconstruction help an organization achieve excellence?

_____
_____
_____
_____
_____

How would you define intentional leadership in your own words? Why is it important?

_____
_____
_____
_____
_____

How can challenging seasons actually aid us and our organizations?

_____
_____
_____
_____
_____

> ### Reflect on
>
> 2 Chronicles 9:12:
>
> *King Solomon gave the Queen of Sheba all she desired and asked for; he gave her more than she had brought him. Then she left and returned with her retinue to her own country.*

Consider the scripture above and answer the following questions:

Why do you think King Solomon was so generous with the Queen of Sheba?

_____
_____
_____
_____
_____
_____

What tangible and intangible gifts did she take back to her own country?

_____
_____
_____
_____
_____
_____
_____
_____

chapter 2

EXCELLENCE IN THE DETAILS

Attention to details shows you actually care about what you do, who you are serving, and who you do it with.

Reading Time

As you read Chapter 2: "Excellence in the Details" in *That Doesn't Just Happen*, review, reflect, and respond to the text by answering the following questions

Review, Reflect, and Respond

What are some details your organization could improve on?

_____
_____
_____
_____
_____
_____
_____
_____
_____

Have you ever noticed inattention to detail when you've visited another establishment? How was it manifested?

_____
_____
_____
_____
_____
_____
_____
_____
_____

How can minor details by themselves add up and become a detriment to your organization?

_____
_____
_____
_____
_____
_____
_____
_____
_____
_____
_____
_____

What does it mean to truly care about what you do? How do you show it?

_____
_____
_____
_____
_____
_____
_____
_____
_____
_____
_____

How can you promote a culture of excellence to your staff?

_____
_____
_____
_____
_____
_____
_____

Do you care about those you serve, or is it all about profits? How do they know that?

_____
_____
_____
_____
_____
_____
_____

Why is having people in the right positions equally as important as having the right people?

_____
_____
_____
_____
_____
_____
_____

> ### Reflect on
>
> Colossians 3:23:
>
> *Whatever you do, work at it with all your heart, as working for the Lord, not for human masters.*

Consider the scripture above and answer the following questions:

How do you interpret Colossians 3:23?

_____
_____
_____
_____
_____
_____
_____
_____

What does it really mean to work at things with "all your heart?"

_____
_____
_____
_____
_____
_____
_____
_____

How do you know when you and other people are working "for the Lord?"

chapter 3

EXCELLENCE IN THE CURATION

Whether a business, a non-profit, a church, or other organization, without leadership setting the pace in creating a culture, the people working there will haphazardly create one.

Reading Time

As you read Chapter 3: "Excellence in the Curation" in *That Doesn't Just Happen*, review, reflect, and respond to the text by answering the following questions.

Review, Reflect, and Respond

What does curation mean to you? How is it important?

_____
_____
_____
_____
_____
_____
_____
_____
_____

Without curation, what do you think your organization would look like? What would it look like with more intentional, advised curation?

_____
_____
_____
_____
_____
_____
_____
_____
_____

Do you think it's important to be patient when it comes to curation, or should it be prioritized?

_____

_____

_____

_____

_____

What happens when you aren't intentional in forming a culture in your organization?

_____

_____

_____

_____

_____

Why is it important to deal with tensions in an organization quickly? What happens when they're not dealt with in a timely manner?

_____

_____

_____

_____

_____

_____

Why is change so difficult for some people? Is this a necessary difficulty?

What value does clarity have in change and curation? How can you offer those you lead more clarity?

Reflect on

1 Kings 6:37-38:

The foundation of the temple of the LORD was laid in the fourth year, in the month of Ziv. In the eleventh year in the month of Bul, the eighth month, the temple was finished in all its details according to its specifications. He had spent seven years building it.

Consider the scripture above and answer the following questions:

Does seven years seem like a long time to build a temple?

_____
_____
_____
_____
_____
_____

Why do you think it took King Solomon this long?

_____
_____
_____
_____
_____
_____

What does this show about King Solomon?

___

chapter 4

EXCELLENCE IN THE CULTURE

When it comes to spreading a contagious culture, sometimes you must act quickly, knowing in the long run it will be worth the effort.

Reading Time

As you read Chapter 4: "Excellence in the Culture" in *That Doesn't Just Happen*, review, reflect, and respond to the text by answering the following questions.

Review, Reflect, and Respond

How would you describe your current organization's culture?

_____
_____
_____
_____
_____
_____
_____
_____
_____

If you could change one thing about the culture, what would it be?

_____
_____
_____
_____
_____
_____
_____
_____
_____
_____

How do you think a negative company culture can hurt the people who work there along with the people the company serves?

_____
_____
_____
_____
_____
_____
_____

Describe the cultures of communities and organizations that exist in your life. What are aspects that you do and don't like?

_____
_____
_____
_____
_____
_____
_____
_____
_____
_____
_____

Explain how culture can be easily changed or a drawn-out process.

_____
_____
_____
_____
_____

How do communication and culture come into play with each other?

_____
_____
_____
_____
_____

How do you think customers, guests, and patrons can sense a negative organizational culture? How do they show they sense it?

_____
_____
_____
_____
_____
_____
_____
_____

Reflect on

1 Timothy 4:12:

Don't let anyone look down on you because you are young, but set an example for the believers in speech, in conduct, in love, in faith and in purity.

Consider the scripture above and answer the following questions:

Why do you think Paul gave Timothy these specific instructions?

_____
_____
_____
_____
_____
_____

How does a person set an example in each of the following areas: speech, conduct, love, faith, and purity?

_____
_____
_____
_____
_____
_____
_____

PART 2

SEE LIKE THE QUEEN OF SHEBA: CREATIVE ADAPTATION AND CULTURAL CONTEXTUALIZATION

chapter 5

SEE THE HARD TRUTHS

What people say about your business is critical to your business.

Reading Time

As you read Chapter 5: "See the Hard Truths" in *That Doesn't Just Happen*, review, reflect, and respond to the text by answering the following questions.

Review, Reflect, and Respond

How is feedback (both positive and negative) from those you serve valuable to your organization?

_____
_____
_____
_____
_____
_____
_____
_____
_____

When have you ignored negative feedback that your organization received? What were the results?

_____
_____
_____
_____
_____
_____
_____
_____
_____

How can your organization collect feedback in a more efficient and effective way?

_____
_____
_____
_____
_____

When you hear feedback requiring a response, does it become a priority to fix it, or does it go on the backburner?

_____
_____
_____
_____
_____

How valuable are first impressions? How can you maximize first impressions?

_____
_____
_____
_____
_____
_____
_____

How can a company's reputation be affected by its leaders response to feedback?

How can following up benefit the guests' experiences?

Reflect on

1 Kings 10:4-56:

When the Queen of Sheba saw all the wisdom of Solomon and the palace he had built, the food on his table, the seating of his officials, the attending servants in their robes, his cupbearers, and the burnt offerings he made at the temple of the LORD, she was overwhelmed.

Consider the scripture above and answer the following questions:

Even though she had great expectations of King Solomon coming in, why do you think the Queen of Sheba was speechless?

_____
_____
_____
_____
_____
_____

What did Solomon's presentation reveal about the grandeur of the God he served?

_____
_____
_____
_____
_____
_____
_____

chapter 6

SEE THE POTENTIAL

The way you carry yourself and the hard work and determination in which you operate speaks volumes to people.

Reading Time

As you read Chapter 6: "See the Potential" in *That Doesn't Just Happen*, review, reflect, and respond to the text by answering the following questions.

Review, Reflect, and Respond

Why might humility be one of the more important traits for a leader to have?

_____
_____
_____
_____
_____
_____
_____
_____
_____

Do you consider yourself humble? How do people approach you with correction?

_____
_____
_____
_____
_____
_____
_____
_____
_____
_____
_____
_____

When have you ever offered advice only to be shut down? Do you think this came from a lack of humility?

_____
_____
_____
_____
_____
_____
_____

When have you ever gotten defensive when you've received advice? What happened?

_____
_____
_____
_____
_____
_____
_____
_____

What areas of your life are you prideful in, if any?

_____
_____
_____
_____

How can pride unchecked be a detriment to an organization as a whole?

_____
_____
_____
_____
_____

How does humility in leadership affect the rest of the organization?

_____
_____
_____
_____
_____

Reflect on

1 Kings 3:7-9:

Now, Lord my God, you have made your servant king in place of my father David. But I am only a little child and do not know how to carry out my duties. Your servant is here among the people you have chosen, a great people, too numerous to count or number. So give your servant a discerning heart to govern your people and to distinguish between right and wrong. For who is able to govern this great people of yours?

Consider the scripture above and answer the following questions:

What stands out to you about this prayer?

_____
_____
_____
_____
_____

If you were to pray this about your organization, what changes might you see?

_____
_____
_____
_____
_____

PART 3

FINISH BETTER: CULTIVATING LEGACY

chapter 7

BUILD TO CHANGE

When it comes to technological advancements, global economic demands, or just the simple conveniences and preferences of a tech-savvy generation, agility and pivoting are critical to survival.

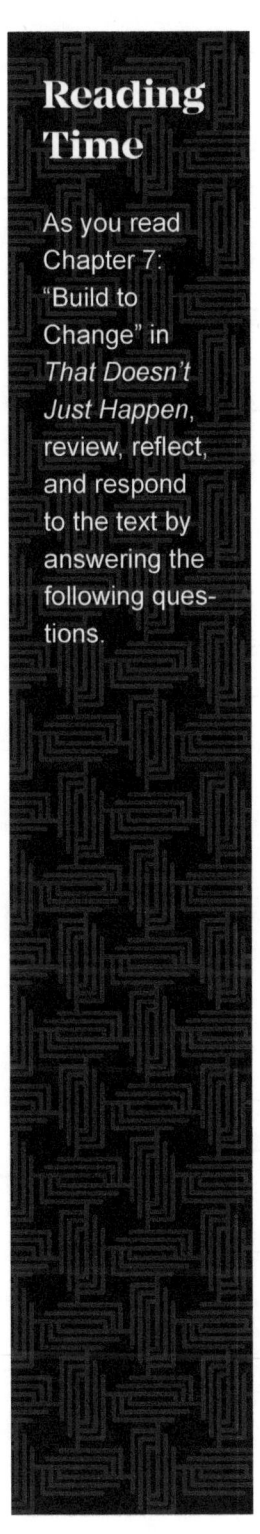

Reading Time

As you read Chapter 7: "Build to Change" in *That Doesn't Just Happen*, review, reflect, and respond to the text by answering the following questions.

Review, Reflect, and Respond

How can one "build to change?" What does this look like in your context?

_____
_____
_____
_____
_____
_____
_____
_____
_____
_____

What's right and wrong about the following statement: "If it isn't broken, don't fix it?"

_____
_____
_____
_____
_____
_____
_____
_____
_____
_____

How have you or your organization pivoted or transitioned in a time of crisis?

What happens if we don't build to change? Is our organization doomed to fail, or can it survive?

Of the corporations and organizations and their transitions discussed in this chapter, which one stood out to you and why?

_____

_____

_____

_____

_____

Do you think pride can piggyback on our successes to the point we don't want to change?

_____

_____

_____

_____

_____

Of the "Five Organizational Phases" discussed in this chapter, what phase do you think your organization is currently in and why?

_____

_____

_____

_____

_____

Reflect on

Proverbs 18:12:

Before the downfall the heart is haughty, but humility comes before honor.

Consider the scripture above and answer the following questions:

How have you seen Proverbs 18:12 play out in your culture?

_____
_____
_____
_____
_____
_____
_____
_____
_____

Why is it important that leaders keep an attitude of humility?

_____
_____
_____
_____
_____
_____
_____
_____

chapter 8

BUILD TO LAST

We could do well to learn from the latter half of Solomon's life, so that we can build to last and ultimately, finish better.

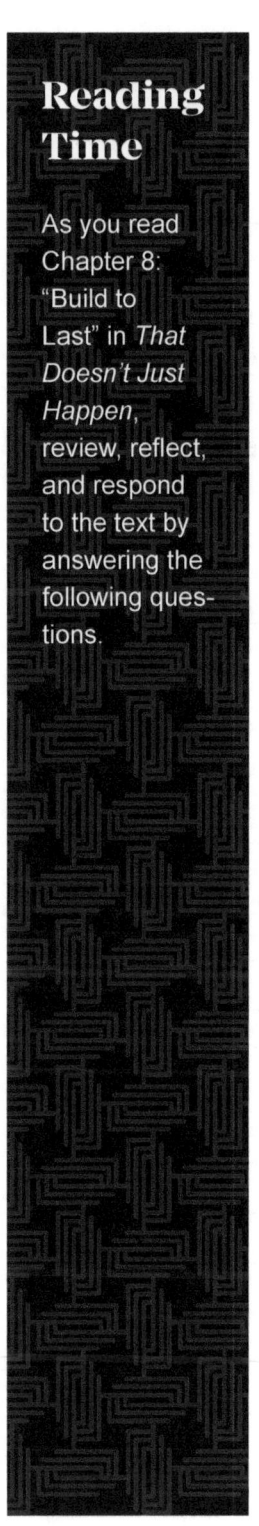

Reading Time

As you read Chapter 8: "Build to Last" in *That Doesn't Just Happen*, review, reflect, and respond to the text by answering the following questions.

Review, Reflect, and Respond

Which is more important: profit or sustainability? Explain your rationale.

_____
_____
_____
_____
_____
_____
_____
_____

What do you think happens if organizations aren't intentional in their longevity and sustainability?

_____
_____
_____
_____
_____
_____
_____
_____
_____
_____

What have you "built to last" in your personal life?

___

How are core values and longevity related to one another?

___

How can a coach or consultant help with sustainability? When have you sought either?

___

How can our views of people affect our organization's longevity? What's a healthy view of those around us?

How can margins help keep us on track? What are some personal margins you have in your life?

> **Reflect on**
>
> Proverbs 11:14:
>
> *For lack of guidance a nation falls, but victory is won through many advisers.*

Consider the scripture above and answer the following questions:

How can you interpret the verse in context of your company or organization?

_____
_____
_____
_____
_____
_____
_____

What does an adviser look like in your life?

_____
_____
_____
_____
_____
_____
_____

How can you advise others?

chapter 9

BUILD TO LEAVE A LEGACY

Enterprise takes vision to see what no one else sees.

Reading Time

As you read Chapter 9: "Build to Leave a Legacy" in *That Doesn't Just Happen*, review, reflect, and respond to the text by answering the following questions.

Review, Reflect, and Respond

What does leaving a legacy mean to you? How important is it to an organization?

_____
_____
_____
_____
_____
_____
_____
_____
_____
_____
_____

What do you hope your legacy is once you're gone?

_____
_____
_____
_____
_____
_____
_____

Does a legacy come naturally, or do we need to be deliberate in seeking it out?

_____
_____
_____
_____
_____

What steps need to be taken when erosion starts taking place within your organization?

_____
_____
_____
_____
_____

Do you think it's important to assess where you are before you start planning on where to go?

_____
_____
_____
_____
_____

What practices can you start implementing today that will gradually aid in getting you where you want to go?

_____
_____
_____
_____
_____
_____
_____
_____
_____
_____

What happens if leaders don't deal with the erosion that's occurring within their organizations?

_____
_____
_____
_____
_____
_____
_____
_____
_____
_____

> ## Reflect on
>
> Matthew 6:20-21:
>
> *But store up for yourselves treasures in heaven, where moths and vermin do not destroy, and where thieves do not break in and steal. For where your treasure is, there your heart will be also.*

Consider the scripture above and answer the following questions:

What kind of treasure can be stored in heaven?

___

___

___

___

___

___

___

What does Matthew 6:20-21 mean when it says, "... there your heart will be also?"

___

___

___

___

___

___

___

How is life different for people who store up treasure in heaven as opposed to on earth?

_____
_____
_____
_____
_____
_____
_____
_____
_____
_____
_____

chapter 10

KEEP ENTERPRISING IF YOU WANT TO KEEP RISING

In order to build something sustainable, you have to begin innovating. Take the time now to enterprise, so you can ultimately finish better.

Reading Time

As you read Chapter 10: "Keep Enterprising If You Want To Keep Rising" in *That Doesn't Just Happen*, review, reflect, and respond to the text by answering the following questions.

Review, Reflect, and Respond

Do you think highly of your personal and organizational potentials, or do you limit their growth?

_____
_____
_____
_____
_____
_____
_____
_____

Define "enterprising" in your own words. What does it look like?

_____
_____
_____
_____
_____
_____
_____
_____
_____
_____

How can constant innovation ensure effectiveness?

___

Is innovation a one-time act or a continual process? Explain.

___

How can culture make or break an organization's growth? Do you think your organization's culture is inhibiting or promoting its growth? How can you tell?

___

Why is sustainability such an important factor in all of an organization's endeavors.

___

What has been your greatest takeaway from *That Doesn't Just Happen*? How can you turn it into an applicable step you take today?

___

Reflect on

1 Corinthians 10:31:

So, whether you eat or drink or whatever you do, do all for the glory of God.

Consider the scripture above and answer the following questions:

What does it mean to do everything for God's glory?

_____
_____
_____
_____
_____
_____
_____
_____

What does this look like in a person's life?

_____
_____
_____
_____
_____
_____
_____

www.ingramcontent.com/pod-product-compliance
Lightning Source LLC
Chambersburg PA
CBHW070208100426
42743CB00013B/3105